2024 Victo

A

MW00883469

Victory Independent Publishing

2005 SE 192nd Ave Suite 200

Camas WA 98607

www.VictoryIndependentPublishing.com

"Those who are happiest are those

who do the most for others."

-Booker T. Washington

"We cannot live only for ourselves.

A thousand fibers connect us with our fellow men."

-Herman Melville

Part I

Getting Seriously Strategic

Chapter 1: Sun Tzu & You

"We know only too well that what we are doing

is nothing more than a drop in the ocean.

But if the drop were not there,

the ocean would be missing something."

- Mother Teresa

With all due respect to Mother Teresa, the amount that is given charitably in the United States each year (around $385 billion from all sources) is larger than the entire Gross Domestic Product (GDP) of countries like Tonga and the Marshall Islands. Though those countries are literal drops in the ocean size-wise, where I come from that is still a lot of money. I'll let you in on a secret: Americans are wealthy and generous. And if you are holding this book, you are likely the latter and probably (by global standards at least) the former.

But what good is our generosity doing? Are the charities to which we give fulfilling our personal mission? Are they reflecting our personal values? Are they making any difference in the real world or are they merely drops in the ocean? The truth is that most of us have absolutely no idea. And it doesn't really need to be that way.

Strategic philanthropy may sound daunting or only for "rich people." In reality, it is a term used to describe the practice of philanthropy where donors use *thoughtful* approaches to maximize the *impact* of their giving. Not so hard, right? It is just a planned and purposeful approach to generosity that seeks to achieve measurable results. Or at least that is what the current literature tells us.

For me, strategic philanthropy may be more than that or less, depending on the donor. Some donors may choose to be hands-on with the organizations they help fund, visiting, cajoling, and encouraging the most effective uses of their donations. Others may just cut checks and never set foot in an Executive Director's or (gasp) Planned Giving Officer's workplace. **Either way can be strategic.** To me, and for the purposes of this book, strategic means *intentionally making choices.* As we will see later, strategy is about evaluating the options for allocating resources.

Once you have done that, you have engaged a problem strategically.

So while it sounds super fancy and therefore out of reach for the average philanthropic giver, nothing could be further from the truth. This is good news, because individuals account for $327 Billion in giving, close to 70% of all donations. That far outpaces giving by corporations, foundations, or bequests. It is also bigger than the GDP of the island nation of Kiribati, but I digress.[1] And even among the bequests, lower-valued estates more than hold their own. Estates under $1 million outgive those in the $1-$10 million grouping and are only eclipsed by the very wealthy in the $10 million and above grouping, where such gifts significantly impact Federal estate taxes.[2]

---

[1] Kiribati, officially known as the Republic of Kiribati, is an island nation situated in the Micronesia sub region of Oceania in the central Pacific Ocean. As of the 2020 census, it has a permanent population of over 119,000, with more than half residing on the Tarawa Atoll.

[2] Giving USA the Annual Report on Philanthropy: www.givingusa.org/

In other words, charitable giving is *not* the exclusive playing field of organizations with huge staffs churning out impact reports or SWOT analyses. Nor is it the particular turf of the family office for the richest household in town. Nope, the heavy philanthropic lifting is being done by people who live in your community, your neighborhood, and even your home. And most don't give much thought to where the money goes and why. Think about it, you probably have a retirement plan. (At least I hope so.) And you probably have investment plans to fund those retirement plans. You may even have tax plans to reduce your overall outlays to Uncle Sam. But statistically speaking, NO ONE has a plan for what may be one of the top spending priorities after the mortgage is paid and food is on the table.

The opposite of strategic is random or uncalculated. I'm quite sure no one thinks of their giving as random, so let's stick with uncalculated for the purposes of our discussion There are over 1.4 million 501(c)(3) organizations in the United States. That number has been growing more or less over the years except for a dip in September 2011. Back then, over 200,000 charitable organizations lost their tax-exempt status. Why? **They failed to file legally required documents for three consecutive years**. If that doesn't make you want to be more intentional and results-driven and ensure that your money is going places that aren't zombie aid organizations, nothing will. I wish you the best. You may stop reading now.

If you are still with me, know this: it's okay if you aren't strategic yet. A wise person once said anything worth doing is worth doing badly...at least at first. But like any startup venture here in the good ole US of A, we can improve our philanthropy with just a little bit of work. Strategic philanthropy is many things, but here are the main points.

- It is a results-oriented way of guiding your philanthropic decisions.

- It is an outcome-oriented lens that can help you decide whether you are achieving your goals or need to update your charitable giving tactics.

- It focuses on the most effective ways to give money to achieve the goals you set for yourself.

Here is a real selling point for those who suffer from donor fatigue, growing tired of continually being asked by organizations with which they have no affiliation, association, or attachment. Strategic philanthropy gives you a rock-solid, respectful, and super polite way to say "no." More on that later.

And yet, most people engage in charitable endeavors at a tactical level. They are asked to donate and think: "Should I cut a check to XYZ?" As we will see, check writing is purely tactical. And while it may be completely logical and in keeping with your intent, in most cases, it happens without much thought. The Chinese philosopher Sun Tzu said, "Strategy without tactics is the slowest route to victory. Tactics without strategy is the noise before defeat." Yes, I am a product of military education, and I first read Sun Tzu in college, well before he became popular in boardrooms, business schools, and airport bookstores.[3]

How do you relate *The Art of War* to philanthropy? Very, very carefully. My point is not to militarize the process of philanthropy or to be jingoistic about it but to provide an organizing philosophy for the importance of strategy before tactics. Sun Tzu's point is that you *can* be successful without thinking through your strategy, but that is the proverbial slow boat to China.

This may seem counterintuitive because strategic thought takes time and brain power. You must know the terrain (the landscape of the problem you want to "attack")

---

[3] You know, just in case you needed a guidebook on how to win the battle for that extra inch of space the armrest with the guy in the middle seat. Hint: "A clever general... avoids an army when its spirit is keen, but attacks it when it is sluggish." Wait for him to go to sleep and then pounce.

and the strengths and weaknesses of your enemy and yourself. If the ultimate goal is making an impact, then strategic thinking gets you there faster and with a better idea of the resources you have at hand. This takes research about the problem you want to solve, the organizations you support, and, most of all, yourself. And that is where we go next.

Chapter 2: Philanthropist, Know Thyself

"If you know the enemy and know yourself,

you need not fear the result of a hundred battles.

If you know yourself but not the enemy,

for every victory gained, you will also suffer a defeat.

If you know neither the enemy nor yourself,

you will succumb in every battle"

- Sun Tzu, The Art of War

How to begin? Well, in many ways, you already have. Enlightened, next-level philanthropy requires money, motivation, and an effective strategy for harmonizing the first two. By continuing with this book, you've demonstrated your motivation. You are inspired to engage in philanthropy at some level. And the world (including Tonga, Kiribati and the Marshall Islands) thanks you. Now, having picked up this book in the first place, I'm willing to wager that you have some money to dedicate to that philanthropic endeavor or a variety of them. (Hey, if you've got money to bet, you certainly have it to donate!) So, we now need to make those dollars match your motivation.

Now, take a deep breath. Seriously, a deep breath followed by a few more to put you in a reflective mood. You may even want to meditate or go for a walk. Whatever it takes to clear your mind and prepare it for the "touchy-feely" part that comes next.

In my financial planning practice, I developed a system to launch the process, and it works quite well with charitable planning, too. Indeed, no matter the *type* of planning, having a deep understanding of where you've been and where you want to go is essential to having the right blueprint in place. Success relies on getting those two items right from the start. Unfortunately, financial matters like philanthropy can be complex, and basic clarity can be hard to find.

I developed my Check Six Client Discovery System™ a series of surveys and interview questions to better understand each person's unique situation. It is a systematic documented method for helping shed light on complicated and vague issues, turning them into well-defined, confident answers. "Check six!" is an aviation term (with which I have some personal history) meaning to visually clear the airspace behind you, increasing your overall situational awareness and determining what needs to be done and in what order. Sound familiar? It's exactly how planning in general and charitable planning in particular should proceed.

The first step in the system is developing a biography. As Shakespeare said, "What's past is prologue, what to come…In yours and my discharge." Understanding and summarizing your past experiences sheds light on what is important to you and how it came to be that way. And it gives you an idea about how you want to shape the future. For instance, one of my personal philanthropic passions is food insecurity. As a young child, my family received food assistance during the economic malaise of the early 1980s. Dad was out of work for quite a while, and I remember vividly the large blocks of cheese and sacks of rice that were the hallmarks of those programs. Well, everyone made it out of that situation just fine. But clearly, my belief in a "hand up" approach to assisting those in need comes from somewhere.

When working with clients, I ask a lot of biographical questions to get a feeling for who they are, where they come from, and how they became the people they are today. Do not skip this step if you are working with this book as a do-it-yourselfer. Sure, you know your own biography, but having a written guide will be helpful. I suggest doing this a little differently on your own.

Ready? Sit down and write your own obituary. Do it in long form. Think of a half-page in the Wall Street Journal where they recap some business tycoon's life, not the local paper's three-sentence blurb. Cover your early formative years and how you were brought up. Talk about how this shaped you into the person you are today.

Here are some questions to guide you:

- Tell me about yourself. Where did you grow up? How did you get to where you are today?

- Describe your immediate & extended family.

- Tell me about your profession and career.

- What is the secret to your success?

- Who had the biggest effect on your life?

- Tell me about your interests.

- What do you like or prefer to do with your time?

- If money were no object, what would you do?

- What type of philanthropist are you? Active? Passive? Why?

I recommend you edit and save this as a document for future reference or print it out and save it with your other planning documents. Planning is a circular process, and we will return to the building blocks later to ensure your outcomes are what we intended. And fear not, the rest of this process is much less macabre.

Chapter 3: Perfect(ing) Vision

"Don let the limitations of others limit your vision.

If you c remove your self-doubt and believe in yourself,

you n achieve what you never thought possible."

- Roy T. Bennett

A Vision Statement describes you, or in this case, your charitable endeavors in a future state of success. It can be a powerful motivational tool. Have you ever found yourself uttering the phrase 'someday I would like to'...? I certainly have. We are, after all, a nation of dreamers. Well, friends, it is time to finish that sentence. In the future, how do you want to spend your time, energy, and money, and on what causes?

It is important to be thoughtful here because it can be difficult, at best, to imagine yourself in the future. This is a topic I deal with quite a bit in my practice. For instance, when working with clients on retirement plans, I have never had a single one say, "I plan to live well into my 90s." And yet, statistically, about 25 percent of them will. When I point this out and emphasize the need to plan for potential longevity, the answer is almost always the same: "That won't be me." This isn't just fatalism or stubbornness on their part. It is the inability to look that far out into the future and see themselves, and it has real-life consequences. Faced with a decision on when to take Social Security benefits, someone without a future self to imagine will always opt to take benefits early, potentially leaving thousands of dollars of income on the table.

So being future-conscious is important for good decision-making. You can hear me talk more in-depth about this topic on The Road Less Babbled (formerly Millennium Manhood) podcast from September of 2021.[4] We evolved from hunter-gatherers with shorter life spans, so it isn't a surprise that we have such a difficult time speculating about the future. As I said on the show, "everything you do that involves your brain and the way you process information is old. It's old technology." How do you upgrade the operating system to consider your future state? Research has shown that the neural activity when thinking about ourselves in the

---

[4] The Road Less Babbled Podcast, Episode 115, Know Your History or Hate Everyone: https://podcasts.spotify.com/pod/show/theroadlessbabbled/episodes/115--Know-Your-History-or-Hate-Everyone-e17cigr

21

future is more like that which occurs when thinking about other people and less like thinking about ourselves. We don't do well with future goals because we aren't even considering the subject as us.

One way to successfully navigate this mental shortcut is to use that to your advantage. In an article in the *Association for Psychological Science* and on the website lifehacker.com, Anne Wilson, a psychologist at Wilfrid Laurier University in Canada, recommends connecting with that third person. She notes that "perhaps the key to being "future-conscious" is making sure that, insofar as our future self feels like someone else, it's someone we love and care about." So, try this exercise with a stand-in for yourself. Choose someone you care about and create your vision statement through their eyes. Or choose an actor to play your part and have them write it. Either way, the important part is to think in terms of the big picture outcomes someone just like you in almost every way (*but certainly not you... wink, wink*) would find satisfying.

You have finished your 'someday sentence.' Are you doing that thing now, or does something need to change to get there? If your someday requires funding, do you have the money? If it requires someone to participate with you, is he or she ready and willing? Spend a few minutes highlighting what resources are available and what needs to be gathered to achieve that vision.

Now, let's get vivid. In his book *Vivid Vision*, author Cameron Herold talks about a vision statement that is "a three-dimensional world that you can step into and explore." Think of it like a pair of virtual reality goggles that you snap on to look around at what you eventually want to create. The author recommends a three-year time frame for this, long enough to see changes but short enough to keep you engaged. Just be prepared to continue doing this exercise every three years as you update your charitable plan, which we will cover in Part III. Here is the structure I recommend for creating your charitable mission statement. Plan on sitting down and writing out at least a paragraph for each.

YOUR WHY: As author and TED Talk star Simon Sinek says, starting with your purpose, cause, or belief is essential when guiding business decisions. And it isn't a bad idea to think of your giving efforts as a business from time to time. You are, after all, using capital (money or time) in order to achieve some result. Of course, the comparison isn't perfect, but neither was the one for a military campaign, per Sun Tzu. So, you know, work with me here. The good news is that completing your biographical history and/or your obit should have helped you identify your why already. If not, it is time to go back and revisit the previous chapter.

YOUR WHO: In three years, who are you helping? Be as specific as you can here, both at the organizational and individual levels. For instance, it is one thing to say that I am helping the local food bank. It is quite another, and I think much more powerful, to say that I am helping the single mother who is running short of groceries every month and wants to be able to feed her two children a wholesome dinner at the end of the day. I would even go so far as to create individual identities, names, and backstories for all of the organizations you work with. Create a document and find photos online to represent these people like an avatar. There is no better way to have crystal clarity on who you want to be helping.

YOUR HOW: Describe in as much detail as you can how you go about helping those you identified above. Do this for all your charities. Are you volunteering? Working on a committee? Donating money? How much time are you spending, and how much money are you prepared to give? It is okay to be audacious here. We will find out later if we can fit the tactics to your desires. A vision statement is a time to dream big, to think about where you want to be, not just where you think it is probable that you will be.

Once you've considered why, who, and how, we move on to two other focus areas: YOUR VALUES and YOUR GOALS. These are big enough topics to deserve their own chapters, but they should be part of the overall Vision document and reviewed and revised accordingly.

Chapter 4: The Value of Your Values

In everything I do, whether in business,

philanthropy, or my personal life,

I am guided by my inner truth, my values."

-Shari Arison

Your VALUES section describes what you believe in and how you want to behave. It defines your deeply held beliefs, attitudes, and principles. What were the key values you were raised with? What values are most important to you today? Maybe you were raised with midwestern values of hard work, family ties, and humility. Or perhaps you are a laid-back west coaster focusing on individuality and healthy living. Maybe you are a mélange (like me) after bouncing around the world in your early years. It really doesn't matter where your values come from; what matters is that you have them, articulate them, and that they are part of your daily life and are subject to change as you (hopefully) mature.

Another way to identify values is to externalize them. Is there anyone you particularly admire for how they have lived their lives? Who and why? What did they think was important, and why does that resonate with you? No one is perfect, so feel free to rope in several people and pick and choose their best traits. You might mash up Mother Teresa, Elon Musk, and Brad Pitt. Or it might be Gary Sinise, Confucius, and Maya Angelou. Find *your* two, three, four, or ten individuals who epitomize your values, and write down what you like about this wholly fictitious person.

Another simple way to highlight your values is to complete the following sentence:

"When all is said and done, the most important things in life are . . . "

Whatever you come up with will be a good starting point for your values.

Finally, if you are struggling, here is a list of values from which to choose. Please don't write me emails or poor reviews because some of these values aren't yours. Remember, it is a menu, not a prescription.

Integrity	Courage	Honesty	Tolerance	Optimism
Environmental Consciousness	Humility	Loyalty	Spirituality	Self-care
Responsibility	Gratitude	Patience	Respect	Adventure
Independence	Generosity	Freedom	Learning	Authentic Relationships
Accountability	Personal Growth	Empathy	Innovation	Justice
Trustworthiness	Family	Self-discipline	Flexibility	Quality
Authenticity	Compassion	Wisdom	Ambition	Mindfulness
Self-expression	Balance	Love	Resilience	Harmony
Fun & Enjoyment	Creativity	Kindness	Teamwork	Perseverance
Open-mindedness	Health	Fairness	Simplicity	Equality

Personal values are just that- personal. They are unique to everyone, and it's important to reflect on what values resonate with you the most. This list serves as a starting point, and you can prioritize, add, or modify values based on your own beliefs and principles.

Once you've chosen your top values, group them together in categories. For instance, Respect, Empathy, and Compassion could potentially fall into a single category and be grouped together. Once you have your groupings, choose the word that best represents the group. This will help give you one central theme for each. As a final step, rank each of your core values in order. There shouldn't be more than four or five singular values after you've gone through this process.

Congratulations, your charitable planning is now more values oriented.

Chapter 5: Goals=CLEAR PACTS

"You will accomplish far more if you set out

to accomplish something specific."

-Tierney & Fleishman, Give $mart

Now, it is time to get very specific about what you want to change in the world. The secret has been out for some time about donors needing to get more specific with the goals or their philanthropy. I read Tierney and Fleishman's Give $mart while studying the curriculum for the Chartered Advisor in Philanthropy (CAP®) designation in 2016. And there are plenty of other books with titles like *Giving Done Right* and *Money Well Spent* that continue encouraging donors (usually large ones) to tackle specific goals.[5]

This naturally led to using the framework of SMART (Specific, Measurable, Attainable, Relevant and Time-Bound) to set philanthropic goals. The concept of SMART goals was introduced in the early 1980s by George T. Doran, a consultant and former Director of Corporate Planning for Washington Water Power Company. The idea

---

[5] Give Smart By Thomas J. Tierney & Joel L. Fleishman, Public Affairs, 2012. Giving Done Right by Phil Buchanan, Public Affairs, 2019. Money Well Spent by Paul Brest & Hal Harvey, Stanford Business Books 2018.

behind SMART goals is to provide a framework for effectively setting and achieving objectives. Over time, the concept of SMART goals has evolved, and variations such as SMARTER (adding Evaluate and Revise) or SMART-ER (adding Ethical and Recorded) have emerged to enhance the goal-setting process.

Indeed, there are several alternative frameworks to SMART goals with snazzy acronyms. To capture the intricacies of a charitable plan I have blended two of them together below. Sure, the self-improvement gurus can stick with their SMART goals, but when it comes to charitable intent, I encourage you to make your goals into CLEAR*PACTS.

Collaboration— Identify who will be involved to make your goal a reality. Many philanthropically inclined folks want their family to be involved in their endeavors. What responsibilities will each person have? Do you expect any inputs, progress reporting, or other information from the specific charity? Who will provide that? Are they aware and willing? This is a good time to identify any potential outcomes that depend on someone other than you.

Limitations—What are the limitations and boundaries that need to be observed? These can be time, financial, or other personal boundaries. How involved are you willing to be before you say 'when." Many charities are starved for money and volunteers and won't hesitate to continue asking for either or both. If you don't set your own boundaries, someone will set them for you.

Emotion—— How emotionally invested are you in the goal? What about the others you've identified as collaborators? The answer for everyone involved should at least be "somewhat," or they may not be worthy of collaboration. However, now is also a good time to admit if you are too emotionally involved to make unbiased decisions and determine if others might be as well. The time is also suitable to ask yourself if the disappointment of failure will create an oversized effect on your psyche or your financials. Either would be a potential red flag.

Appreciable— Realistically, how big of an influence will your donations have on the chosen charities? Given your emotional attachment, how big of an impact will it have on you? How big of an impact on your budget or estate plan? It's okay to admit that your contributions won't move the needle much, but you can seek matching opportunities or other ways to be more impactful.

Refinable—How will your involvement change and why? What adjustments might need to be made if the goal isn't reached or takes longer than projected? How can you polish these goa￼ over time to make them shiny and new so that you rema￼ engaged?

Purpose￼—Which of your values identified in the previous ￼eps does this goal align with? If the answer is none, the￼ is something wrong with your strategic planning or your g￼l. Now is the time to figure this out and make changes t￼ your planning.

Actions–￼What actions will further your progress toward your goal￼ I find it easiest to create a numerical list. But remembe￼we are not talking about tactics here. The actions you ident￼y here should be broad steps you are willing to take to m￼t the goal. You may take some or none of these actions, b￼ that is a decision left to the discussion of tactics in Part 2.

Continuity—Is this a long-term goal seeking continuous improvement? A shorter-term goal to meet a quantifiable need? Or a one-and-done goal?

Trackable— The biggest issue I have with SMART goals is the measurable part. Large benefactors may be able to break out the statistics related to their gifts and thereby measure their impact. But it isn't really feasible for us members of the 99% club. Instead, tracking can be simplified to a series of questions and a scoring system about the gifts you are making. By consistently using the same questions to track your charitable goas, you can simplify the monitoring process and gain a clear understanding of your achievements. This approach provides a structured framework for evaluating your efforts, adjusting, and ultimately increasing the effectiveness of your charitable endeavors. These questions should be specific and tied to you as the donor as well as the organizat n. A scoring system like the one that follows is a must.

Assign a ore of 1 to 5 points for each, with 1 meaning that you stron y disagree with the statement and 5 meaning that you stron y agree.

1. I   ve a strong relationship with _____.

2. T y have an increased impact on _____ thanks to their prog mming.

3. I   d being associated with _____ to be personally rewardin

4. I   el that _____ appreciates my contributions to their mis n.

5. M donations have had an impact on _____ that is observab

6. _   ___ has short-term, and long-term goals that are well-esta ished and align with my philanthropic vision.

7. An acceptable amount of my donation goes directly toward fulfilling _____ mission.

8. I receive frequent updates from _____ regarding how my money is used and what results are generated.

9. All the board of directors at _____ contribute their own funds to meet the organizational goals.

Scoring:

- 0-15 points- Back to the drawing board.

- 16-30 points- Your charitable relationship may be on life support, and it is time to see if your dollars could go further by going elsewhere.

- 30+ points- You have a solid relationship with a good institution. Keep on keeping on!

Specific—The most significant strength of the SMART goal system is keeping things as specific and granular as possible. So, let's keep that in mind as you review what you've come up with during this process. Synthesize all the informati 1 you've gathered for each category into a single sentence.

A an example, here is how I created a CLEAR* ACTS matrix for my involvement with a local food ban]

( )llaboration	*My family is involved, occasionally volunteering. This is a good way to continue to introduce my son to charitable endeavors and the responsibilities of citizenship. I am the main participant, providing funds and volunteering time and expertise.*
] **mitations**	*Money. Time. Time comes at the expense of other activities, and it is necessary to balance this with family life.*
] **notional**	*Highly emotional, given family history. However, it is not so emotional that it will negatively my personal affect happiness.*

Appreciable	*Contributions are comparatively moderate, but the impact measured by numbers of meals served is significant to me.*
Refinable	*Very flexible. I can volunteer and help in numerous ways and can donate time or money to various internal projects.*
Purposeful	*Fulfills my personal values of gratitude, empathy and optimism.*
Actions	*1. I can volunteer as part of the finance committee or fundraising committee.* *2. I can contribute to their capital campaigns.* *3. We can volunteer as a family during distributions.*
Continuity	*This is a long-term goal with numerous*

	short -term payoffs.
Trackable	*Current score = 38*
Specific	*To help reduce food insecurity in my local community through volunteerism, fundraising and financial donations.*

Chapter 6: Mission Possible Statement

"Working hard for something we do not care about is called stress, working hard for something we love is called passion."

-Simon Sinek, Start with Why

After clarifying your values, vision, and goals, it is time to channel your inner Jerry Maguire and develop a Mission Statement. If you need to Google that reference, avoid confusing it with another Tom Cruise movie and wind up with a Mission Impossible Statement. That would completely contradict the spirit and intent of charity. After all, we are here to solve problems, not purposely tilt at windmills.

A Personal Mission Statement is a concise and powerful declaration that encapsulates who you are, what you stand for, and what you aim to achieve. It provides clarity, direction, and a sense of purpose in guiding your choices, actions, and overall life journey. Your mission should be expressed in how you live your life. The idea here is to clarify and summarize in an easily digestible format. Keep it simple, clear, and brief. This is a chance to summarize all of your goals into a single sentence that guides you.

A mission statement should address:

- Why do I exist, and what drives me?

- On what do I want to focus my time and treasure?

- Who do I want to become as a person and a philanthropist?

- How do I intend to make a positive difference in the lives of others, my community, or the world at large?

- What unique strengths, talents, skills, and qualities do I bring to the table to serve my mission?

Your mission statement should evolve over time as your values change, but it should always remain positive. Your mission (should you choose to accept it) is not to avoid things but to move forward towards something. Here is a relatively simple formula for starting that you can customize and tweak to get the desired result.

1. Let's choose an opening statement that best fits your personality.

It is my/our **desire** to
It is my/our **job** to
It is my/our **mission** to
It is my/our **responsibility** to
My/our **challenge** is to
My/our **first priority** is to
My/our **goal** is to
I/we **envision**
I/we **exist** to
I/we are **committed** to
I/we **strive** to
I/we **will**

Other

2.   What do you most want to do? Choose an action that you are willing and want to take:

Achieve	Improve
Build	Make
Coordinate	Maintain
Create	Promote
Change	Provide
Develop	Pursue
Disseminate	Store
Empower	Supply
Enhance	Support
Foster	Utilize

Achieve	Improve
Impact	Other

3.   To affect this:

Balance	Improvement
Compassion	Attention
Care	Responsiveness
Growth	Service
Support	Living conditions
Innovation	Other
Faith	

4.   For whom? Or what?

Myself

Others
Our family
Our community
The world
Children
Animals
Charitable causes
Our friends and family
The underprivileged

5.   And... (You can choose more than one. This is optional, but you may have more than one person or group who are part of your mission.)

Myself
Others
Our family
Our community
The world
Children
Animals
Charitable causes
Our friends and family
The underprivileged

6.   How? What action (or actions) will you commit to
in order to achieve your mission?

Using
Expending
Contributing
Utilizing
Giving
Donating
Other

7.   What resources will you dedicate toward your

mission?

Skills
Abilities

Money
A combination of things
Power
Talents
Knowledge
Experience
Something else

8. Some questions to ask yourself now that you have a draft:

- Does your mission statement challenge and motivate you?

- Does it bring out the best in you?

- Does it communicate your vision and values?

- Does it address significant roles in your life?

- Does it represent your unique contribution to society?

A Sample Charitable Mission Statement: We are committed to improving living conditions and access to the arts in our local community through gifts of money, time, and experience.

That was easy…right?

Part 2: Talking Tactics

Chapter 7: Big Picture Tactics

"The life of a man consists not in seeing visions

and dreaming dreams, but in active charity

and in willing service."

-Henry Wadsworth Longfellow

As discussed in Part 1, strategy and tactics are two concepts often used interchangeably, but they have distinct differences. Strategy refers to the overarching plan or approach to achieving a specific goal, while tactics refer to the specific actions or steps taken to execute that plan. A strategy is a high-level plan that outlines an organization's or individual's overall direction and goals. It involves choosing where to allocate resources, how to compete in the marketplace, and how to achieve long-term success. A strategy is typically broad and long-term, providing a framework for making decisions and taking action.

Tactics, on the other hand, are the specific actions taken to implement the strategy. They are concrete steps taken to achieve short-term goals and objectives. They are usually more detailed and focused than strategy and are often adjusted in response to changing circumstances.

In summary, strategy is the plan for achieving a goal, while tactics are the specific actions taken to execute that plan. Both strategy and tactics are important for achieving success, but they require different skills and approaches. A good strategy provides a clear direction and purpose, while effective tactics help to bring that strategy to life. Understanding the difference between strategy and tactics is key to developing a comprehensive and successful plan for achieving your goals.

Let's start by gathering what you will need for this process. Depending on how organized you are, this could take some time. Fear not, I'll be here when you get back.

- Tax returns

- Donation receipts

- Financial Plans-Retirement, Cash Flow, Tax

- Brokerage Statements

- IRA and Employer Account statements

- Mortgage documents

- Current gift arrangements or pledges

- Current estate documents (wills, trusts, etc.)

The tactical questions boil down to the questions of when to give and what. And these questions will, for better or worse, lead to further questions. Let's start with the first question: When do you want to give? Quite simply, are you looking to give now, in this lifetime? Do you want to see your good works in use? Do you want to visit the facility you helped fund? Are you aiming to serve out the meals you helped buy? Or are you looking to use your assets in life to fund your lifestyle? And when you are gone, have the remainder fund your charitable endeavors? The answer (or answers, as we may blend a little now with more later) will drive how you look at your assets and what and when you want to contribute to the cause.

For instance, what if you want to make a gift without altering your current cash flow? Cash is king. And cash flow is the kingmaker. Suppose you want to make potentially significant gifts without affecting your current lifestyle. In that case, we are likely talking about one of two things: continuing to make occasional contributions as usual and/or contributing something after you go to the Great Philanthropic Gala in the Sky.

The answer could be as simple as addressing your estate planning and adding your preferred charity as a Beneficiary, designated on one of your accounts. Designating preferred charities in wills, living trusts, and retirement plans will allow you to support your favorite charitable causes without affecting assets during your lifetime. Your financial picture doesn't change. What's yours is still yours., until you die. Please, oh please, on behalf of the charities to whom you will leave your bequests, have this conversation with your family or other beneficiaries before making the switch. And be sure to document your decision-making with a written charitable plan. Nothing is worse for an organization than having a gift challenged after the fact. It looks and feels bad for everyone involved.

The second question is what you will give. We talked about cash and beneficiary designations as timing issues. If you decide to give more than cash now, you need to brush up on the following tactics. And if you decide to make bigger gifts that benefit both you (through taxes or otherwise) and the charity, then you really need tactical, and probably legal, help.

A quick note on taxation. Tax savings should never be the primary driver in any charitable giving plan.[6] Charitable giving, meaningful and productive, should be the primary driver. Rare is the case where someone without charitable intent or desire would be better off financially by instituting a plan of giving. Indeed, if anyone knows one, I would love to hear about it. But tax savings are nice, too. And probably, there is some correlation between the generosity cited at the beginning of this book and the

---

[6] Good news! It usually isn't. Surveys done by US Bank indicate that tax savings are around 5th in a list of reasons why donors give.

structures of the tax code. You might as well be rewarded for doing some good in the world. And you should get all of the good out of it that you can, which is where the strategy part of the discussion gets really interesting.

In the following chapters, we will examine strategies for giving, from the easiest to the most time intensive.

Chapter 8: Show Them the Money

"Cash is king."

-Unknown

When it comes to charitable giving, cash isn't just king—it's the monarch, emperor, and supreme overlord of donations. Cash donations make up the bulk of annual gifts because they're just so darn convenient. Swiping your card or signing a check is easy, and the money lands in the charity's account faster than you can say "philanthropy," ready to do good right away.

And though tax reasons aren't primary, they are certainly worth mentioning as your donations will be deductible on your income taxes for up to sixty percent of your Adjusted Gross Income. Of course, this is only if you ITEMIZE YOUR DEDUCTIONS. If you are among the 99% of taxpayers covered by the expanded standard deduction, then your deduction is ZERO.[7]

Cash contributions offer the advantage of immediate and tangible impact. The liquidity of cash enables the swift

---

[7] Under current tax laws which sunset December 31st, 2025. If you ar reading this after that date, the tax treatment is anyone's guess. Consult a professional. Operators are standing by.

deployment of resources for the intended charity. The charity can immediately use the money to respond to urgent needs or keep their projects running smoothly—it's philanthropy on demand! This immediacy proves valuable when responding to urgent needs or sustaining ongoing initiatives, contributing to the overall efficiency of charitable efforts. But it is also stressful for charities that live 'hand to mouth' on cash contributions.

Cash contributions provide adaptive flexibility. I refer to cash as "Namaste Philanthropy" as, like a yoga instructor, it can stretch and bend to fit any charitable goal, keeping pace with the ever-changing charitable landscape. The inherent flexibility of cash contributions allows for responsiveness to evolving charitable goals.

Beyond the warm fuzzies, cash donations come with some sweet tax perks. Claiming deductions might even make doing your taxes a bit more tolerable. The ability to claim tax deductions serves as an additional motivator, enhancing the overall impact of philanthropy.

Cash contributions often result in immediate recognition and engagement with supporting organizations. This recognition may enhance the overall engagement experience for contributors, at least those who are not averse to a public pat on the back.

Finally, there is the often untapped potential for matching. Does your employer have a charitable matching program? If they're a bigwig like a Fortune 500 company, chances are they do. About 65% of Fortune 500 companies have them, but smaller firms may too. Over 26 million people are covered by some type of matching gift program. Unfortunately, up to $7 billion in potential matching funds are estimated to go unclaimed each year, dwarfing the $2-3 billion actually used. Who doesn't like free money?[8]

---

[8] See https://doublethedonation.com/matching-gift-statistics/

Of course, there are drawbacks to cash contributions. Nothing is ever perfect, and cash might not have the best long-term overall influence on operations. Cash donations usually come out of your daily budget, so they might be more modest in size and have a lower potential for lasting or sizeable impact.

And, while cash donations can reduce your current income taxes, their smaller size may mean that they don't qualify you for itemized deductions on their own. Given that nine of ten taxpayers take the standard deduction under current tax law (as of 2024), your cash contributions may not be helping you at all with your taxes. Even if they do, the deduction is capped at a percentage of your Adjusted Gross Income, so there's a limit to the financial kudos you can score.

Cash is certainly king, and no charitable organization will turn its nose at it, but it may not be the tactical solution many donors seek.

Chapter 9: Show Them the Money (From Your IRA)

"No one is useless in this world who lightens the burdens of another."

-Charles Dickens

In the realm of charitable giving and financial planning, there's a hidden gem that many IRA owners might not be fully aware of – the Qualified Charitable Distribution (QCD). If you are in or approaching your 7th decade, this is a tool you need to understand and utilize as much as possible to make tax-advantaged gifts. This strategic tool can enhance your philanthropic efforts and fine-tune your financial plan.

A Qualified Charitable Distribution is a direct transfer of funds from an Individual Retirement Account (IRA) to a qualified charitable organization. This maneuver is unique because it allows IRA owners who are 70½ years or older to contribute funds directly to charity, bypassing the need to count the distribution as taxable income. This is both huge and hugely underutilized.

The QCD is like cash donations on steroids. It has all the perks of cash contributions plus some extra magic. One of the standout perks of QCDs is their tax efficiency.

It's like a tax Houdini act—directly transferring funds to a qualified charity allows IRA owners to exclude the distributed amount from their taxable income while still satisfying their Required Minimum Distribution (RMD) obligations. Poof! No taxes on the amount transferred!

Since the distributed amount is excluded from taxable income, it doesn't count toward AGI calculations. This can have ripple effects, like reducing the taxation of Social Security benefits and improving certain deductions tied to AGI.

With the beefed-up standard deduction these days, many taxpayers find themselves utilizing this option instead of itemizing deductions. QCDs offer a strategic advantage here, allowing IRA owners to benefit from their contributions to charities while still taking the standard deduction. This has been a game-changer for many of my clients who are adjusting their retirement plans once they hit the RMD age.

QCD+, An Enhanced Giving Strategy

Do you dream of making your charitable contributions feel like hitting the lottery jackpot? Here's a genius move: use your QCD to pay life insurance premiums on a policy owned by your favorite charity. It's like turning your mandatory RMDs into a financial rocket booster, propelling your generosity into the stratosphere. Imagine your modest QCD contributions growing into a future mega-gift where your hard-earned pennies turn into dollars.

Here's the playbook: If you've been a regular donor, your charity might qualify for life insurance on you. Or, take the bull by the horns and get the policy yourself, then gift it to your charity. You might secure a term policy before hitting the RMD stage, keeping costs low. Once RMDs start, switch to a permanent policy and hand it over to the charity. Just remember, the benefits must go straight to the charity—no sneaky perks for you, or you'll lose any tax benefits you thought you'd receive.

The charity can use your QCD donations to pay the life insurance premiums. When you shuffle off this mortal coil, the policy's death benefit goes straight into the charity's coffers. If all goes well, only a fraction of your QCD will be needed for premiums, leaving the charity with extra cash. Plus, the life insurance policy will act as a financial safety net for them. They can borrow against it, giving them even more wiggle room before you bid this world adieu. Win-win, anyone?

Of course, every rose has its thorns. QCDs have all the disadvantages of cash contributions plus one major stipulation. QCDs are only for those who've hit the grand old age of 70 ½. So, if you're younger, you'll just have to wait your turn.

QCDs might have some quirks, and you need to be meticulous about your record-keeping, but they can pack an extra punch with your charitable giving.

Chapter 10: Don't Be Daft, Fund a DAF

"Where there is charity and wisdom,

there is neither fear nor ignorance."

-Francis of Assisi

In the realm of charitable giving, Donor-Advised Funds (DAFs) have emerged as powerful tools, offering individuals and organizations a strategic and flexible approach to philanthropy. In 2022, Donor Advised Funds allocated $52 billion in grants. These funds combine simplicity, tax advantages, and a streamlined process, making them an increasingly popular choice for donors seeking impactful ways to contribute to causes they care about. Buckle up if this is the first you've heard about Donor Advised Funds. Expect to hear more, much more about this amazingly flexible and increasingly powerful tool for philanthropy.

A donor-advised fund (DAF) serves as a philanthropic vehicle established within a public charity, which operates as the sponsoring organization overseeing individual DAF accounts. Under this arrangement, donors make irrevocable contributions to their respective DAFs, entitling them to an immediate tax deduction. Once funds are deposited into the DAF, donors have the discretion to recommend grants to qualified charitable organizations at their discretion. Contributions to the DAF may be made at the donor's convenience, allowing for flexibility in the timing of charitable giving. Furthermore, any investment growth generated within the DAF is tax-free, enhancing the overall philanthropic impact of the fund. This tactical structure facilitates strategic philanthropy by enabling donors to centralize their charitable contributions, receive tax benefits, and strategically allocate grants to support their preferred philanthropic causes.

With a DAF, you can drop a hefty lump-sum donation all at once, smoothing out your giving process. This lets you sprinkle your generosity over multiple charities over time while reaping immediate tax deductions. You can donate more than just cash—think appreciated securities, real estate, or those weird assets you don't know what to do with. It's a tax-saving buffet where you choose what to donate and how large of a tax deduction you want (or need) upfront.

And there is potential for tax-free growth. DAFs provide investment options, enabling donors to grow their charitable assets, thereby increasing the overall impact of their funds. Larger funds can be professionally managed as part of your overall investment plan.

For those who prefer their philanthropy to be on the down-low, DAFs offer the option of anonymous giving. And DAFs offer the flexibility to recommend grants to various charitable organizations, allowing donors to respond to emerging needs or evolving priorities. You can easily adapt to new causes or shift priorities, aligning your giving with your ever-evolving goals, vision, and values. DAFs are the Swiss Army knife of philanthropic giving, a multipurpose tool for all kinds of donors.

Want to turn charity into a family affair? DAFs are perfect for involving the whole gang. It's a great way to instill and pass on your values. Hold a family meeting, let everyone pick their favorite charities, and decide on donations together. It's more fun than a Netflix binge, and you might even learn something about each other.

Don't forget about your final act of generosity. If you have a Donor Advised Fund, naming charities as final beneficiaries can end up as a major gift depending on how you invest and direct grants from the fund. These designations provide flexibility and can be modified as circumstances change. Basically, make sure that when you die, whatever is left in your DAF finds its way to the right places.

The disadvantages of the DAF are often overlooked, and one is that the IRS is scrutinizing their status. Be sure to stay updated as new regulations are promulgated. Other issues include the limited control over investments. If you're a smaller donor, your control over investments might be limited. While DAFs offer various investment options, you might not get the same customization as you would with other investment vehicles.

DAFs, like any other investment vehicle, may have administrative fees for managing the fund, which can nibble away at your charitable impact. Consider it the cost of doing philanthropic business, but those fees can still be annoying.

Finally, be sure to monitor changes in tax law. Lumping your contributions into a single year to itemize your deductions and get a bigger tax break in that year makes a lot of sense unless the tax law goes back to pre-2017 when the standard deduction was much smaller and easier to itemize. And all Congress needs to do to make that happen is what they are best at doing…nothing. The law automatically sunsets at the end of 2025.

No matter the scope of your philanthropy, the DAF is a solid tool for making your charitable giving both impactful and efficient. But some changes may be afoot.

Chapter 11: Give Your Stuff Away

"The necessity of life is to find your gift.

The purpose of life is to give it away."

-Pablo Picasso

What do classic cars, RVs, and boats have in common? Yes, they are all vehicles, thank you, Captain Obvious, but they are also assets that tend to sit around after the post-purchase honeymoon period, gathering dust and sometimes leaking oil. Along with parcels of land that remain stubbornly in the middle of nowhere and vacation properties where no one vacations, they would fall into the category of unwanted or unused assets whose disappearance from your personal balance sheet would not affect your income. How about that Apple stock you bought at $1.50 back when it was just a computer company? If you sell it, you will be slapped with significant capital gains and probably slapped by your tax preparer. Unless you need the dividends (see cash flow), then removing the stock and donating it eliminates the capital gains tax and can create a meaningful charitable donation. Occasionally, getting rid of an unused asset will actually *help* your cash flow if it requires upkeep, insurance, or the like. So, consider immediate gifts of appreciated stock, business interests, life insurance, real estate, or personal property as outright gifts or in conjunction with a Donor Advised Fund or the tactics outlined in the coming pages.

A word of warning, though. Before dragging your lightly used vehicle into your favorite charity's parking lot (literally or figuratively), check with the charity you are considering for potential gifts. Have them review their gifting policy and ensure they accept your gift before committing to it or drafting documents. Charities can differ in their approach to assets like real estate and closely held stock. It isn't fun for them to have to disclaim a gift after you are gone and in no position to work out a resolution.

Donating personal property to a registered charity can mean deductions, potentially reducing taxable income. Basically, you remove items from your driveway and estate and can get a current-year deduction for them. Donating personal property can declutter your home or office, creating a more organized living or working environment. You can also avoid being featured on the next season of Hoarders. It's like spring cleaning with a financial reward.

There may also be some potential appreciation, beneficial to the organization. Some items you donate, like artwork or collectibles, might go up in value over time, making your donation even more beneficial to the charity. Of course, if that happens, you won't see a dime—your tax deduction is fixed at the time of donation. But hey, you can still brag about your excellent taste!

One major drawback with personal property donations is the appraisal challenge. Determining the value of certain items for tax purposes can be complex. You'll likely need professional appraisal services, and guess who gets to foot that bill? Yep, it's you.

And let's face it, Marie Kondo and her KonMari Method™ be damned, some personal property comes with significant emotional attachment.[9] Parting with personal belongings, especially those with sentimental value, can be tougher than you think. Once it's gone, it's gone. So, make sure you're really ready to let whatever it is walk out your door.

Finally, not all charities are interested in your vintage lava lamp collection or your slightly creepy doll assortment. This means your donation options might be a bit restricted. Ask about their acceptance policies before you make your decision on what to part with.

Donations of personal property can be worth the extra effort necessary, but they will require a fair amount of work upfront to be completed without undue stress.

---

[9] I'm kidding. She's wonderful and tidying up and being more mindful of what you own is good advice.

Chapter 12: Home Sweet Home?

"Service to others is the rent you pay

for your room here on earth."

-Mohammed Ali

Your home is not just your castle. It is likely the largest asset you own. And that, in a day and age where children rarely need or want to take over Mom and Dad's abode, can make it a significant charitable asset. If you like the idea but prefer to keep a roof over your head until your final days, consider a Retained Life Estate.

You transfer the title to your residence or vacation home to the charity. You continue to live in or use the property for life or a specified term of years and continue to be responsible for all taxes and upkeep. The property passes to the charity, which sells it for a nice profit. Your kids and grandchildren can then visit the facility you helped fund with your extremely generous donation and bask in your glorious memory.

The advantages of a retained life estate include financial flexibility. You can give the charity a significant asset but retain the security of using your property for the rest of your life, and you will receive an immediate income tax deduction for a portion of the appraised value of your property. You can terminate your life estate at any time and move out. If you do, you may receive an additional income tax deduction. Or you and the charity may jointly decide to sell the property and prorate the sale proceeds.

There is also the matter of estate efficiency. When you're gone, your kids or other heirs won't have to deal with the headache of selling the house and divvying up the proceeds. You've already done the heavy lifting for them.

However, it is important to remember that life estates are typically irrevocable, meaning donors cannot easily change or revoke the arrangement once it is established. Life estate arrangements can involve legal complexities and administrative burdens, requiring careful planning and execution. Life estate agreements may lead to conflicts among beneficiaries or disagreements with the charity over property management or usage. And, of course, determining the property's value for tax purposes may require professional appraisal services, incurring additional expenses. There is also the legal expense of drafting the agreement properly. However, doing it right is essential to avoid the aforementioned issues with beneficiaries.

A major gift that has zero effect on current cash flow and may streamline your estate settlement, a retained life estate is a way to utilize your largest asset and not burden your heirs with its sale process.

Chapter 13: Recognize & Annuitize

"He who wishes to secure the good of others

has already secured his own."

-Confucius

This and the following few chapters describe tactics that generally fall into the category of Income-Generating Charitable Gifts—gifts that provide a tax deduction and a stream of income to the donor. Charitable Gift Annuities are the gift that keeps on giving... to you! You hand over some assets, usually cash or securities, to a charity, and in return, they promise to send you a fixed stream of income for life. They usually have a minimum donation requirement because, you know, they're not running a yard sale. In exchange for the donation, the charity agrees to pay the donor a fixed income stream for life, typically through periodic payments (e.g., monthly, quarterly, or annually.) The annuity payments are fixed and predetermined based on the donor's age at the time of the gift.

The amount of income the donor receives is determined by the annuity rate, which is based on factors such as the donor's age and prevailing interest rates at the time of the gift. Generally, older donors receive higher annuity rates. Donors may be eligible for immediate income tax deductions in the year of the gift, based on the present value of the remainder interest that the charity will receive upon the donor's death. After the donor's lifetime, the charitable organization retains the remaining assets in the annuity fund to support its mission and charitable activities.

Reliable income for life and immediate tax deductions sounds pretty good, right? Plus, you might dodge some capital gains taxes on appreciated assets. In other words, nothing new here other than the stream of income that is created to come back to you.

Setting up a charitable gift annuity is relatively straightforward compared to other planned giving vehicles, with fewer administrative requirements. Some may even allow for splitting the annuity contribution among several charities.

Of course, consider the irrevocability of a charitable annuity. Once you set it up, there's no going back. And those fixed payments don't adjust for inflation, so plan ahead.

And make sure to do your homework on the solvency of the organization. Donors should ensure that the charitable organization offering the annuity is financially stable and capable of fulfilling its obligations over the long term. If they go under, so do your payments. Most smaller charities use outside providers for this, so be sure to vet them as well.

For donors seeking tax advantages and cash flow, a charitable annuity might be a good fit for their overall income and tax plans. However, it requires some forethought and shouldn't be the only source of income given the lack of inflation protections.

Chapter 14: Everybody Into the Pool

"You give but little when you give your possessions.

It is when you give of yourself that you truly give."

-Kahlil Gibran

A charitable pooled income fund (PIF) is a charitable giving vehicle that allows donors to contribute to a pooled fund managed by a charitable organization, typically a university, foundation, or other nonprofit institution. It is a bit like a giant charitable piggy bank where everyone tosses in their spare change—only this piggy bank is managed by a university, foundation, or other nonprofit, and the spare change includes cash, securities, or real estate. Here's how it works: donors contribute their assets to the pooled fund, which is combined with other donors' contributions into one big investment pot. The charitable organization takes it from there, investing the pooled assets in a diversified portfolio that might include stocks, bonds, real estate, or other investment vehicles.

The beauty of a PIF is that it generates income over time. This income is regularly distributed to the individual donors or their designated beneficiaries, typically quarterly or annually. Think of it as getting a slice of the pie you helped bake. Upon the death of the last income beneficiary or at the end of a specified term, the remaining assets in the pooled income fund are transferred to the charitable organization to support its charitable purposes.

A PIF is another way of creating an income stream. Think of it as getting a steady allowance but for grown-ups. Donors or their chosen beneficiaries receive regular income from the pooled fund, providing financial security and peace of mind.

Pooled-income funds are managed by experienced investment professionals, often with access to institutional-quality investment strategies and expertise. Thus, the fund is managed by experienced investment pros who probably know a bit more about investing than your cousin Jerry, who swears by cryptocurrency and still lives in your aunt's basement. Or maybe not. Be sure to do your homework.

Pooled-income funds offer diversification benefits, as the assets are invested across a range of asset classes and securities, reducing investment risk. Depending on the sophistication of the management, additional risk management strategies may also be used. And shouldn't we all pay a little more attention to risk management?

Donors are again eligible for immediate income tax deductions based on the present value of the remainder interest passing to the charitable organization. Additionally, capital gains taxes on appreciated assets may be reduced or deferred. Uncle Sam will have to find his lunch money elsewhere.

Irrevocability will again be an issue. Pooled-income funds may have minimum contribution requirements, and donors should ensure they have sufficient assets to meet these requirements. Similar to creating a CRT, this may require professional guidance from financial advisors, estate planning attorneys, and tax experts. That's a lot of cooks to create one dish.

Think of a PIF as a way to make your money work for you while you work for a good cause. Which just may be your recipe for success.

Chapter 15: A Matter of Trusts

"No one has ever become poor from giving."

-Anne Frank

A charitable remainder trust (CRT) is a planned giving arrangement that allows individuals to support charitable organizations while providing themselves or their beneficiaries with income for a specified period or for life. here are two primary types of charitable remainder trusts. In a Charitable Remainder Unitrust (CRUT), the income payments are calculated as a fixed percentage of the trust's value, revalued annually. This means that if the trust's value increases, the income payments also increase, providing potential inflation protection. Or a Charitable Remainder Annuity Trust (CRAT) where you receive fixed income payments, regardless of how the trust's value changes. It's like having a steady paycheck that doesn't change, no matter what happens in the stock market, and it potentially means a larger remainder for your charity of choice.

In either case, the donor establishes a charitable remainder trust by transferring assets, such as cash, securities, real estate, or other valuable property, into an irrevocable trust. The trust is managed by a trustee, which could be the donor, a financial institution, or another designated party. The trustee is responsible for administering the trust according to the terms set forth in the trust agreement. The trust agreement specifies a fixed percentage of the trust's value to be paid out to the donor or other named beneficiaries, either for a specified term of years or for the lifetime of the beneficiaries. Upon funding the trust, you get an immediate income tax deduction based on the present value of the charitable remainder interest that will eventually pass to the designated charitable organizations. After the specified income period ends or upon the death of the last income beneficiary, the remaining assets in the trust (the charitable remainder interest) are transferred to one or more charities designated by you.

Charitable remainder trusts allow donors to support charitable causes with potentially sizeable gifts. And they do it while providing for their own financial needs and those of their loved ones. You receive a reliable income stream for you or your beneficiaries, either for life or for a specified term. With most pensions a thing of the past, a reliable stream of income is usually a welcome addition to a comprehensive financial plan.

You enjoy immediate income tax deductions based on the present value of the charitable remainder interest and potential reductions in capital gains taxes on appreciated assets used to fund the trust. Avoiding two (potentially three if your estate is large enough) taxes is smart tax planning.

Like membership in some of the world's secret societies, you are in once you are in. Charitable remainder trusts are typically irrevocable, meaning you can't change the terms. They can also be quite complex to set up and manage, often requiring professional guidance from that same all-star team of estate planning attorneys, financial advisors, and tax experts. Plus, charitable remainder trusts often have minimum funding requirements, so you need to ensure you have sufficient assets to make the trust effective.

If you want to simplify your financial life in the short term, this may not be the right move. But in the long run, it may be just the right tactic. Perspective is important, as are prior planning and good advice.

Part 3: Performance Enhancement

Chapter 16: I Believe You Can Fly

"I have always found that plans are useless,

but planning is indispensable."

-Dwight D. Eisenhower

Now, it is time for you to leave the proverbial nest and go out into the world to do good. Or more good. Or even, more good...better. To fly on your own toward a better tomorrow filled with strategic and tactical philanthropy. But wait...as Vince the Sham Wow Guy said in his ubiquitous infomercial of the early 2000s...there is more.[10]

Thinking strategically and using the tactics we've discovered is just the beginning of the process. Plans are a useless collection of outdated assumptions and guesswork the instant the ink dries. But *planning* is a refinable process of continual assessment and improvement on the uncrowded highway toward greatness. Forget the noun and focus on the verb form and suddenly, you are in a continuous cycle of planning, acting, and reviewing. Or, as we used to say

---

[10] I actually met the man himself at a boat show in Oakland, California. I was pitching securitized financing for new watercraft; he was selling $10 towels. Guess who did more business that day?

another lifetime ago when I was a young Naval Flight Officer: Brief, Fly, Debrief.

I had forgotten the old mantra until one day, as a nascent small business owner, I had the pleasure of sitting in on a presentation by Anthony Bourke, the CEO & Founder of Mach 2 Consulting. In 2018, he shared his message of peak performance with a few hundred advisors at a conference in Washington, DC. Anthony, callsign "AB," has over 3,000 hours of flight time in various high-performance aircraft and was one of the first pilots to fly an F-16 in homeland defense efforts over New York City in the aftermath of September 11th.[2] He was based in California at the time and found himself trapped on the East Coast during a business trip as air traffic shut down. Seeing that something was terribly wrong he called his squadron commander to ask, "How Can I Help?" He quickly figured out that there was an F-16 squadron on the other side of the field and volunteered to fly homeland defense over New

York City with the 134th Fighter Squadron of the Vermont Air National Guard. A very cool customer, and if you get the chance to hear him tell that story, I challenge you not to get goosebumps.

AB brought me back to something I had learned as a young backseater in the F-14 Tomcat, callsign Baby Huey, with a couple of thousand hours of my own in tactical aircraft as well as a couple of hundred carrier-arrested landings (take that AB!)[11] He reminded me of the feedback system aircrews created and nurtured to ensure continuous improvement and peak performance. If you want to take any endeavor to the next level, you must plan, execute, and review your progress. Brief, Fly, Debrief. If it sounds vaguely familiar, it may be because AB has shared his message of peak performance with more than 1,000,000 people in twelve countries. You certainly didn't hear it from

---

[11] See, I told you. Neither original nor cool. But still better than my initials. Sorry, AB.

the previously mentioned Tom Cruise in one of the Top

Gun movies.

Chapter 17: Brief, Fly Debrief

"Philanthropy, to me, is being engaged, not only with your resources but getting people and yourself really involved and doing things that haven't been done before."

-Eli Broad

Anthony (AB) used the example of the Blue Angels, renowned for their precision aerial maneuvers and their employment of the "Brief, Fly, Debrief" mantra to ensure safety and excellence in performance. The Blue Angels, the U.S. Navy's flight demonstration squadron, were formed in 1946, making them one of the oldest formal aerobatic teams in the world. They are renowned for their precise, high-speed aerial maneuvers, performed by six demonstration pilots. Their shows, which include breathtaking formations and solo routines, are seen by millions of spectators annually in the U.S. and around the world. The Blue Angels have become a symbol of naval excellence and aviation prowess, representing the skill, dedication, and teamwork of the U.S. Navy and Marine Corps. [12]

---

[12] Yes, yet another military anecdote. But if you can think of a better example of achieving high performance, I'm all ears. Check out the 2024 Blue Angles documentary on Amazon Prime Video to remove any doubts.

Here is how team members systematize their schedule to enhance performance and achieve greatness, and how you can, too.

Brief: Team members gather for a comprehensive briefing session before each flight. Pilots review the flight plan, objectives, and safety protocols while discussing potential challenges and contingencies. Clear communication and alignment are essential to ensure everyone understands their roles and responsibilities. Pilots use visualization techniques to put themselves in the cockpit before even suiting up. They move their hands on imaginary throttles and call out on imaginary radios. They fully engage themselves in what is to come.

By completing the exercises in chapter one, you visualized what success would look like in your charitable giving. Then, you moved on to align the roles and responsibilities through your choice of tactics. You should feel fully briefed and ready to go—because you are.

Fly: During the flight, pilots execute meticulously choreographed maneuvers with precision and synchronization. Each member relies on extensive training, situational awareness, and teamwork to perform their maneuvers flawlessly, captivating audiences with their aerial displays.

Go forth and captivate the people and causes you care about with your display of compassion and good citizenship. But be sure to maintain your situational awareness, ready to critique your own performance and the performance of others.

Debrief: Following the flight, the team conducts a thorough debriefing session to assess the performance. Pilots provide feedback on what went well and areas for improvement, facilitating a culture of continuous learning and refinement.

Lessons learned during debriefs are integrated into future practices to enhance performance and safety.

Now, the real magic happens. You take something that seemed perfect to the untrained eye and tear it apart mercilessly with the goal of improving it. Seek out information and feedback to learn from mistakes and refine your strategy and tactics as necessary. Then, do it all over again. Allow me to quote myself again, this time from the My Worst Investment Ever podcast: "In that debrief, we are going to talk about everything you did well and everything you didn't do well because it is the only way you learn and it is the only way you get better. You've got to debrief the failures."[13]

While the strategic planning processes of charitable giving and the Blue Angels' mantra of Brief, Fly, Debrief

---

[13] Upon reading the name of the podcast, you can tell that I practice what I preach about coming clean in the debrief. Listen to Andrew Stotz's interview with me for My Worst Investment Ever, Episode 493- Patrick Huey – Learn to Apply "Brief, Fly, Debrief" to Your Life: https://myworstinvestmentever.com/ep493-patrick-huey-learn-to-apply-brief-fly-debrief-to-your-life/

differ in context and application, they share fundamental principles:

1. Mission Focus: Both approaches emphasize the importance of clarity in the mission or objective, ensuring that actions align with overarching goals. Do your homework. Know yourself. Imagine what the future will bring.

2. Preparation: Thorough preparation is essential for success, whether planning philanthropic initiatives or aerial performances. This includes assessing needs, refining tactics, and addressing potential challenges.

3. Continuous Improvement: Philanthropists and flight demonstration teams recognize the value of continuous learning and adaptation. Or at least they should. Regular evaluation and feedback loops enable them to refine their approaches and enhance effectiveness over time. Too often in planning (retirement, investment, tax, or charitable giving), we tend to gloss over what didn't go well. No more. Be honest, be successful, and continue to get better. I really do believe that with the right strategies, tactics, and continual improvement mindset, you, too, can soar beyond your wildest dreams.

Patrick Huey is a CERTIFIED FINANCIAL PLANNER™ professional, Chartered Advisor in Philanthropy®, and an Accredited Tax Preparer. He earned a bachelor's degree in history from the University of Pittsburgh and a Master of Business Administration from Arizona State University.

Email him at: patrick@victoryindependentplanning.com

Made in the USA
Columbia, SC
24 July 2024

38634024Π00065